Chomper Champs

by Gary Miller

TM
sundance
A Haights Cross Communications Company

sundance

A Haights Cross Communications ◆⁻ Company

Published by
Sundance Publishing
P.O. Box 740
One Beeman Road
Northborough, MA 01532–0740
800-343-8204
www.sundancepub.com

Chomper Champs
ISBN 0-7608-9359-4

Illustrations by Matt Phillips

Photo Credits

cover (pancakes) Tom Schierlitz/Getty Images, Inc., (boy) Steve McAlister/Getty
Images, Inc.; p. 1 ©Ted Spiegel/CORBIS; p. 6 ©Jeffrey L. Rotman/CORBIS;
pp. 6–7 ©Todd Marshall; p. 8 Everett Collection, Inc.; p. 9 ©Ted Spiegel/CORBIS;
p. 10 (giant crocodile) ©Reuters/CORBIS, (refrigerator) ©Royalty-Free/Corbis;
p.11 ©Reuters/CORBIS; pp. 12–13 ©Jim Zuckerman/CORBIS; p. 16 Richard Ellis/Photo
Researchers, Inc.; p. 18 ©Clive Druett, Papilio/CORBIS; p. 19 ©BOOL DAN/CORBIS
SYGMA; p. 20 ©Mark Moffett/Minden Pictures; p. 21 ©Ken Schafer/CORBIS;
p. 25 Chris Hondros/Getty Images, Inc., (hamburgers) ©Mark Cooper/CORBIS;
p. 26 Chris Hondros/Getty Images, Inc.; p. 27 ©Shannon Stapleton/Reuters/CORBIS;
p. 28 Jeff Fusco/Getty Images, Inc.; p. 29 Jeff Fusco/Getty Images, Inc.; back cover
(left) ©Todd Marshall, (right) Richard Ellis/Photo Researchers, Inc.

Printed In Canada

Table
of Contents

Jurassic Chomp!

Jaws six feet wide! Teeth like sharpened spears! Run for your lives!

These chompers aren't alive today. Be glad they aren't. For some of these hungry monsters, a human would be just the right size for a snack!

Marine Mega-Muncher

If you think the great white shark is scary, try the megalodon. This mega-shark was probably two to three times longer than the biggest great white shark. It may have weighed more than ten times as much.

The megalodon needed something big for its main course—so it ate whales! The giant shark attacked from below, using its almost seven-inch teeth. It may have chomped off a flipper first, then gone in for the kill!

Open Wide!

Scientists compared megalodon teeth to the teeth of today's sharks. They used these comparisons to build a model of a megalodon jaw.

Megalodon jaw

Big Gulp!

Tyrannosaurus rex stood about as tall as a two-story house. Its strong back legs carried it along at up to 25 miles per hour. That's much faster than you could run.

T-rex loved king-sized meals. It ate up to 150 pounds of meat in one bite. So, imagine how much meat it ate in a single day! Such a big appetite could cause problems. One **fossil** had a lump of food stuck in its throat. The monster muncher probably choked to death.

Hey! How'd that thing get so big?

Dino-stars?

In 1940, the makers of the movie *One Million B.C.* made dinosaurs by sticking fins on crocodiles, lizards, and iguanas. Then they filmed them close up to make them look giant!

Is it lunchtime yet?

Tyrannosaurus rex model

Q: What happens when dinosaurs drive?

A: *Tyrannosaurus wrecks!*

Swamp King!

As the sun comes up, a large plant-eating dinosaur drinks calmly from a swamp. Suddenly, a giant crocodile jumps from the water. The croc's teeth grab the dinosaur's leg, and it becomes the croc's breakfast.

Model of a giant croc

Millions of years ago, the giant crocodile was the king of the swamp. And no wonder! The croc's jaws were longer than a person is tall. And from nose to tail, the giant crocodile was more than twice as long as the biggest SUV!

Giant croc

Today's croc

This gold necklace really compliments my complexion.

Welcome to Crocodopolis!

Ancient Egyptians worshipped a crocodile god. And in the town of Crocodopolis, Egyptians kept tame crocodiles. People fed the crocs sweet cakes. They even decorated the crocodiles with jewelry—but carefully!

Giant Vegetarian

Not all dinosaurs were **predators**.
Take the brachiosaurus, one of the biggest
dinosaurs ever. When it was time for dinner,
this big lizard headed for the salad bar at
the top of the forest!

The brachiosaurus stood taller than a
four-story building. It weighed as much as
20 elephants. When it ate, this chomper
tore branches and leaves from the treetops.
This giant **vegetarian** probably ate about
400 pounds a day. That's a lot of salad!

And for Madame, the all-you-can-eat salad buffet!

Brachiosaurus, 40 feet tall

Giraffe-osaurus?

Brachiosaurus has a lot in
common with giraffes of today.

	Brachiosaurus	Giraffe
Long neck	✔	✔
Leaf eater	✔	✔
Herd traveler	✔	✔

Giraffe, 18 feet tall

Man, 6 feet tall

Alive and Dangerous!

Some big chompers are alive today!

Forget those munching monsters of long ago. These beastly biters are chomping their way around our planet right now!

So, watch out. You don't want to get bitten!

Monster Mash

Giant squid and sperm whales are natural enemies. Sperm whales love to eat squid—including giant squid. So when these two monsters meet, it's often a fight to the death.

In 1965, the crew of a Russian ship had ringside seats for this rarely seen matchup. The whale chomped the squid. The squid fought back with its long **tentacles**. Both fighters lost. The squid squeezed the whale to death. But the squid died, too. Part of its head was found in the whale's belly!

My money's on the whale!

See these natural predators in a rare fight to the death!!

	Sid the Squid	Whomper the Whale
Weight	1,900 pounds	106,000 pounds
Length	60 feet	62 feet
Secret Weapon	Squeezing tentacles	Crushing jaws and teeth

Its Drool Rules!

The Komodo dragon is the largest lizard on Earth. It can kill with its sharp teeth. But if this lizard king's fierce bite doesn't kill you, its spit will. Germs in its **saliva**, or spit, are deadly.

American Lizard King

The Gila monster of the southwestern United States has a poisonous bite, too. When this 20-inch lizard chomps its prey, it injects poison along its teeth that usually finishes off most victims.

So even animals that escape the dragon's bite get sick and die later on. Then the Komodo sniffs them out and eats them.

At nine feet long and 300 pounds, this Indonesian reptile is the size of a big alligator. It can eat a deer in one meal. It has even been known to bite humans!

Why do they call him a dragon?

Have you smelled his breath?

Honey, Who Ate the Rainforest?

We did!

Leaf-cutter ants live in **colonies**, or groups, of up to eight million ants. Piece by piece, a colony can chomp the leaves off a whole tree. That might sound harmless. But there are millions of these colonies in Central and South America.

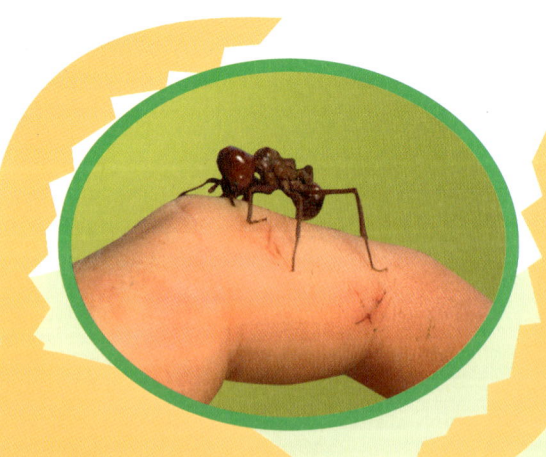

Strange Medicine

What do you do in Costa Rica when you cut yourself? Some people say you can use leaf-cutter ants to close the wound. When you place ant heads onto cuts, the ants bite down. Their pincers close the cuts and stay in place like temporary stitches.

> One tree down, only 4 million to go!

Leaf-cutter ants eating a leaf

A colony of leaf-cutters can destroy all the plants on a farm. They munch through trees in jungle forests and in towns and cities. That leads to billions of dollars in damages each year!

Human Chompers!

I can't believe I ate the whole thing!

Well, these chomper champs did! They ate hot dogs, pies, cakes, and more. Bring the food, and these champs will chomp. And they eat fast, so watch your fingers!

Gut Busters

Every year, **competitive** eating contests take place in cities around the world. Big crowds show up to see who can eat the most chicken wings, hot dogs, hamburgers—and lots more.

Sometimes these chompers eat foods that are a little—well—unusual. Try beef tongues and quail eggs! Anybody like some reindeer sausage? Or how about some yummy cow brains? Champion eaters chomp all these foods. No wonder the winners sometimes go home with stomachaches!

One too many hot dogs?

Leave It to the Pros!

Eating contests are not just fun and games. They are for adults only, and they can be dangerous. That's why there are medical teams at all International Federation of Competitive Eating (IFOCE) events.

Q: Why is it easy to win a turkey-eating contest?

A: *All you have to do is gobble!*

Man Bites Dogs!

CONEY ISLAND, NEW YORK—JULY 4, 2004
The biggest eaters in the world were ready.
Ice cream eating champ Cookie Jarvis was
there. So were burrito champ, Badlands
Booker, and Crazy Legs Conti, the king of
green bean chomping. It was time for a
famous hot dog eating contest held each
year in New York City!

Eat 53.5 hot dogs in 12 minutes? No problem!

Takeru at the hot dog eating contest

TAKERU KOBAYASHI

TAKERU KOBAYASHI

HOME: Nagano, Japan
AGE: 24 WEIGHT: 132 pounds

WORLD RECORDS

COW BRAINS
57 (17.7 pounds) in 15 minutes

HOT DOGS
53.5 Hot dogs and buns in 12 minutes

RICE BALLS
20 pounds of rice balls in 30 minutes

EATING TIP: Takeru breaks each hot dog in two, then stuffs both parts into his mouth.

In the end, the big boys lost to a little guy from Japan. Takeru Kobayashi ate 53.5 hot dogs in just 12 minutes! That beat the second-place eater by more than 15 dogs.

Watch out! That guy is on a roll!

Woman Bites Back!

Most competitive eaters are men. But one woman gives the guys a real stomachache. She's 36-year-old Sonya Thomas. Sonya only weighs about 100 pounds. But she can outeat men four times her size.

Yikes! Chicken? I'm out of here!

Sonya at chicken wing eating contest

In Sonya's first year as a chomper champ, she won thirty thousand dollars in prize money. By the middle of the year, she held twelve world eating records!

Her nickname is "The Black Widow." Why? Because she's named after the spider that munches on male spiders.

Q: What does a spider eat with her hamburger?
A: French flies!

CHOMPER CHAMP

SONYA THOMAS

SONYA THOMAS

HOME: Alexandria, VA
AGE: 36   WEIGHT: 106 pounds

WORLD RECORDS

CHEESECAKE
11 pounds in 9 minutes
CHICKEN WINGS
167 in 32 minutes
HARD-BOILED EGGS
65 in 6 minutes, 40 seconds

FEEDING FACTOID
To burn off all that food, Sonya runs for 2 hours a day, 4 days a week!

2003
EATING ROOKIE
OF THE YEAR

So, ANYBODY want a hot dog now?

Fact File

A blue whale does not have teeth. But that doesn't stop it from eating about 4 tons of food a day!

One kind of caterpillar eats 86,000 times its own weight in its first 56 days of life! That would be like a human baby eating 273 tons of food.

He can't stop eating!

The world's biggest one-day barbecue happened in Australia. More than 44,000 people ate 300,000 sausages, 100,000 steaks, and 50,000 chicken burgers!

The Japanese love chomper champs. Competitive eaters there can win hundreds of thousands of dollars in a year.

Glossary

colonies groups of animals of the same kind that live together

competitive being in a contest or in a struggle to win

fossil a trace of a plant or animal that has been kept from rotting by being buried in earth or preserved in rock

predators animals that hunt other animals for food

saliva the clear liquid in the mouths of animals and humans

tentacles the long, armlike parts that stick out from the bodies of some animals, such as squid and octopuses

vegetarian a person or animal that eats only plants and plant products

Index